I WANT *to Be Me*

Stop Wearing the Mask

Rachel Solace

BALBOA.PRESS
A DIVISION OF HAY HOUSE

Balboa Press books may be ordered through booksellers or by contacting:

Balboa Press
A Division of Hay House
1151 W. 2nd St
Bloomington IN 47403
www.balboapress.co.uk
UK TFN: 0800 0148647 (Toll Free inside the UK)
UK Local: (02) 0369 56325 (+44 20 3885 6882 from outside the UK)

Print information available on the last page.

ISBN: 979-8-7652-1680-4 (sc)
ISBN: 979-8-7652-1682-8 (hc)
ISBN: 979-8-7652-1681-1 (e)

Library of Congress Control Number: 2026906654

Balboa Press rev. date: 03/17/2026

Special thanks to my friend who has supported me and given emotional support during the making of this book.

Contents

Introduction

This book is mainly about myself and my struggle with fear and anxiety otherwise known as a 'trauma wound' (Howard 2023). The book will hopefully act as a guide to help other people who struggle with emotions and how to express themselves. I became so traumatised as a result of an emotional wound that over the years I ended up destroying myself and felt broken. I did not know how to trust my own instincts or intuition. It felt like there was a block stopping me from saying how I really felt. It has been described by Romano (2026) and Howard (2023) as knowing what is going to happen but as a result of fear you ignore your gut feelings. Your gut feelings are actually your nervous system trying to tell you something. This book is also part of my own therapy even though I had plenty of sessions with different councillors. It is helping me learn through knowledge and wisdom. In fact I think I should have listened to myself a bit more as I have a lot of wisdom as do we all. It's just that we do not have the capacity to realise it at the time. Jung (1916) says "that the privilege of a lifetime is to become who you truly are". I feel that I became so traumatised by certain events when I was not able to say how I really felt. It made me feel small and begin to doubt myself and I became overwhelmed by things. This can be described as a wound that never heals (Smith 2022). In fact, it felt like I was on a big hamster wheel and not knowing how to get off. Furthermore this book is not a self-pitying book but it will help me to learn how to have self-compassion and hopefully it will help me to self-heal.

Chapter One

Fear

I THINK L HAVE ALWAYS STRUGGLED WITH FEAR MOST OF MY LIFE and not feeling good enough, always having to prove my self-worth. This may have been due to the traumatic road traffic accident I had at the age of six. Dispenza (2012) said that traumatic brain injuries may cause your brain to be troubled in later life. I don't know why this fear came about but l was afraid of being shouted at by my parents, especially my mother. l just don't know why she always seemed to be angry with me. I was afraid to answer back in case I got into trouble. At other times mum was very kind and would try and help as much as she could. I didn't like conflict of any kind and was always a very shy girl especially at school. l was very naive about life. I didn't have a real boyfriend until l was nineteen, a soldier, who I thought we would last forever and have children but that turned out to be a waste of time and I just thought naively that was that.

Both of my parents were very protective of me, especially mum and l think that's why l left home to live in the nurses home whilst doing my nurse training. I wanted to feel independent and grown up. I think l felt a bit smothered and wanted to make my own way in the world.

Due to their over protection I became more co-dependent on them and I relied on their support too much. Carl Jung (1916) mentions in his book The Psychology of the Unconscious, that the mothers wound is sometimes a reaction to the fact that she is unhappy and it passes onto you as her unmet needs and desires.

I began to become too overwhelmed by things and feeling other people's emotions. In other words an empath. As an empath you tend to ignore your gut feelings as you don't want to hurt other people and I could feel this with my mum and later my sister and then my dad, in fact I have been overthinking for absolutely years but I didn't realise I was just hyper aware of danger and needed to to over protect myself.

I have learnt that by ignoring your gut feelings you become a people pleaser and it affects your nervous system. I have also learnt that your feelings are a part of you and you need to be yourself to be happy. Don't hide behind a mask, it can have a devastating effect.

This book will be using lots of references from books on self-healing. You will learn to just accept things as they are. Do not try to force things, just stop and think and breathe. Do not let anyone, even your family destroy your peace and rush you into making decisions for you. Don't carry other people's problems, they aren't yours.

My Accident

I really don't remember much about my accident or the life before but I know it was a traumatic brain injury resulting from a road traffic accident when I was a young girl of six. It happened in 1968 and I was hit by a car and hurled up in the air then hitting my head on the road resulting in being unconscious for nearly three weeks. I remember my mum saying that she had asked God for one thing "please save my daughter" and she would not ask for anything else. I don't think mum ever did ask for anything else but it still made her very controlling of my sister and me. The main damage was my brain and nerve damage resulting in me not being able to use my right arm properly without it shaking so I learnt to use my left arm and have been mainly left handed. This did have an effect on my nursing career and would knock my confidence.

Chapter Two

My relationships with men

AS MENTIONED BEFORE I DIDN'T REALLY HAVE A REAL BOYFRIEND until I was nineteen. I guess I didn't really feel comfortable with men. I did have a few dates with men but it was always half in and half out. I thought that relationships would be forever. My relationship with my soldier was not the fairy tale ending l expected. I had stayed faithful to him and while waiting for him to return from his tour of duty in the army and I was left devastated when he told me he had met someone else. l remember crying for about five hours. It felt like my heart was broken. He obviously preferred her. No amount of him trying to console me would work. I was devastated, however l hid my feelings after the crying and pretended it didn't hurt me. I suffered with anxiety and I couldn't control my emotions, O'Morain (2018) described anxiety in adults as not being given the tools to nurture themselves when developing. I remember mum saying that she wouldn't mind if I got serious with my first boyfriend, (although too late) and this led me to believe I needed mum's constant approval and permission to have relationships or even to do certain things. That's probably why

I moved into the nurse's home in another town to try to gain some independence where I had to pay my own rent and look after my own needs.

It took me three years to get over that relationship. It left me confused and hurt. I did have a couple of boyfriends after that but nothing worked due to my anxiety. These relationships didn't last long. I think my fear of abandonment probably looked like desperation but I knew it was my fear that I couldn't cope with. The most painful relationship was with a man called Carl with whom I developed a severe attachment to. It broke my heart when we broke up as I was just so addicted to him. Carl had a profound effect on me and that apart from two brief bad relationships, I haven't really gone out with anyone else for about thirty years. It wasn't until selling the house I loved that I realised what I had been doing to myself. It was a destructive pattern that I had to find out why it kept on happening.

Chapter Three

Mothers Wound - My relationship with my mother

MY RELATIONSHIP WITH MY MOTHER WAS NOT A HAPPY ONE FOR the majority of the time, Once I hit teenage years it just felt strained. Carl Jung (1916) says that a lot of parental wounds are inherited. The mothers wound can feel like emotional abuse and trauma. It can be so stifling and smothering that I felt trapped; however I didn't know it at the time - I just thought it was normal. It felt so claustrophobic that I couldn't really have a life of my own. I think that's why I moved away from the family home when I was eighteen. I felt too afraid to say what I wanted and I didn't like being shouted at, so when I moved to Bristol after working in Blackpool for four years I enjoyed being there and being independent. I was going to stay in the south of England but when I was going to buy a flat in the south west mum asked me why I wanted to live so far away from her. She said would never come and see me and thought I was going to be lonely! Her attitude could have been described as guilt tripping me as described by Dispenza (2012).

Of course I didn't want to hurt mum so I gave up the freedom and choices to live there. I therefore grew up not knowing how to set boundaries. In fact I think I became a 'people pleaser' quite early on in life. I would hold my feelings in. It's easier than confrontation (Howard 2023).

Roxanne (2024) mentions in her book 'How not to break your heart' that when you suppress your emotions it causes inner turmoil. Eventually it causes hurt feelings that fester and then your emotions explode. It also makes you very unbalanced and I became so dysregulated that I was ignoring my own desires and needs. It made me emotionally unstable. I feel that my mum became so over protective and quite manipulative. She became very anxious and perhaps paranoid. Later on she became obsessed with things that had to be done at certain times and was very regimental. Mum would be phoning me up at set times and if I wasn't there to answer the phone then she would go into such a panic. Kelley (2024) mentioned that mothers are the greatest worriers of all. They think it's their job to control things. It gives negative energy. This pattern led me to become anxious and afraid and not willing to take chances. My mother humiliated me several times in front of other people. One time she accused me of not paying her any board money even though I was not living at home at the time. This was in front of her friend and her friend said "oh isn't that terrible", however I did not answer her and correct her or answer back. It made me feel embarrassed and ashamed. I was eighteen at that time and was just starting my nursing career.

So then I moved back to Manchester and got a staff nurse

job in a large inner city hospital where I met the man who broke my heart, and also has been my greatest teacher "a twin flame" (Jung 1916). We were mirroring each other. This has caused me to have anxious attachments to men. Alex Howard in his book 'It's not your fault (2023)', says if you grow up believing you have to earn love and you end up chasing love. Roxanne (2024) wrote that we lack self love and become too vulnerable and unhealthy. Dispenza (2012) says your mother is the key as she was your mirror and you become whatever you need to be by bracing yourself as a means of protection. You act as the inner child, you try to fix everybody's problems and constantly over explain yourself. Daughters of emotionally unstable mothers have 'imposter syndrome', where you feel like you're not good enough and you lack the life skills to move on. (Romano 2016). says also your mother is quite frightened of, perhaps her husband, or men in general. She also said that because your mother stuffed down her emotions they do not recognise that you are having difficulty too. I feel that although I have been attracted to some emotionally unavailable men, or this kind of man was attracted to me, they posed a danger to me, making me frightened. I just adapted in the best way I could. I think this is what I did. Mothers like this also become jealous of their daughters' lives. I felt this a lot, for example if I was dating someone I just felt my mum's eyes on me and I could not relax. I did not think I could have anybody around my place as my mum would say "me and your dad will be round first thing in the morning". I was always being monitored.

I had a good idea that my mother felt abandoned as a child

because her own mother had died when she was fifteen years old. She then could have felt responsible for looking after her younger sister and the house due to her dad working full time. In my own life my mum was always protective of dad and if I said anything about him that she did not like she would fiercely defend him.

Conversely mum would sometimes say “I’m coming to live with you. I’m fed up with my husband. On my days off she wanted to come over and stay overnight making me feel trapped in my own home. Mum even criticised my friends saying it’s always you that makes the effort to go and see them. I actually did not mind doing this as they were my friends and lived quite a distance away. Romano (2016) said your mum’s job is to regulate your husband so that if you say anything about him that she feels is derogatory she will shut you down; and yet I felt she was always running around after him wearing herself out. I could not make mum understand that she should look after herself and so thought I was having a go at her. Mum moods definitely depended on how dad was behaving. Mum did not communicate her needs to dad at all. He was happy to leave that responsibility to my sister and me. Even when dad had cancer of the throat she fiercely defended his smoking, saying there is no proof that smoking could have caused it. Fortunately his throat cancer was caught in time and it was successfully treated. Mum was unaware of how she was treating me and my sister, and dad was only too glad to be left alone to do his own thing. I felt that this left mum quite lonely. It was difficult to make her happy, she just didn’t enjoy herself anymore. There was no sparkle to her. It was like she did not have a life once my sister and I had left home. I didn't realise how she had affected me, keeping me small to the extent that if a man was interested in me I would brush him off, being too afraid of rejection.

Due to the fact that I had retired early from work which was something I later regretted; I felt I had to take burdens off my sister and had to take my fair share of looking after my parents, however these were my thoughts only due to my dysregulated brain. (Dispenza 2012) says that your mind works in opposition and sends mixed signals to your brain, as you may have guilt feelings that could have been instilled by your upbringing. Mothers prevent you from feeling things so when I had feelings for Carl, someone I met and fell in love with, I did not know how to express them properly, and I would say all the wrong things I was so overwhelmed. Howard (2023) says that you shut down emotions as a way of protecting yourself and it also acts as a prison and you don't feel safe. Mum's temper fluctuated so much that I never knew if I was doing the right thing and I would be apprehensive. I thought I needed her permission to do things as I did not want to upset her or make her angry. This is because I think now she was jealous of my life as she never really had one, or so she thought. I could feel her resentment at times and so felt like I was walking on egg shells.

Romano (2016) says you grow up not knowing where your boundaries are and do not know how to handle red flag warnings. If I could have handled red flag warnings better I would not have been so pacified in relationships where you feel people are more powerful than yourself. Bradshaw (1998) explains that a person without boundaries has no limit and is easily confused, wasting a lot of energy.

Bradshaw (1998) further explains that toxic shame can be a soul murderer and can also be complex and disturbing and cause pain, depression and feelings of self doubt. It leads to isolation, loneliness and paranoia, perfectionism and feeling inferiority. It destroys your authentic self and you become a false person. Total self love is the only way to happiness and the love of others. Shame is a natural feeling that allows a person to function well but when the feeling of shame is suppressed by coercive and/or perfectionism the person becomes inherently flawed, inferior and defective and also suffers pain. You disown yourself and you become secretive. The physical pain I was experiencing was mainly in my chest making it hard to get my breath. Jung (1916) explains that the pain you feel is the one where you have denied yourself things as they are like missed opportunities; for instance the opportunity to love and have career fulfilments, not making the best of yourself. I would sometimes not tell my parents and my sister where I was going out because I did not want to over explain myself. When you're shamed you're also embarrassed and when you are in that kind of situation you feel caught off guard and exposed to things that you're not ready for.

A toxic shamed person is divided in him or herself and you cannot offer yourself to another person if you don't really know who you are. I felt so much shame and embarrassment with Carl. The relationship was obviously a toxic one. I think when I lost my mind due to anxiety my behaviour could have been mirroring my mothers behaviour. She was very reactive when she felt she had lost control of any situation. I became quite unapproachable. This may have affected my relationships with family, especially my extremely high anxiety with men. I felt uncomfortable at times especially when I felt under pressure. People who are over sensitive need time to process things. For example when people are rushing you to make a decision it's easy to get confused.

Perhaps I grew up in a toxic family with unpredictable behaviours. When my sister and I were young mum was really lovely and proud of us both. However when we were teenagers mum and dad became very controlling. Mum wanted to know everything, including personal things, about our lives. Communication was very difficult, especially around our social lives. I certainly felt uncomfortable discussing it with her if I was going out with anyone. She even wrote down when our periods were due in her diary. She would say "Don't you dare get pregnant, me and your father won't be looking after your children". They would both stay up when my sister and I went out for the evening until however late we got home. It instilled fear in me and that's why I had become so secretive about some parts of my life. There was no respect for our privacy. She also would criticise me and humiliate me in public places like in the supermarket over little things; for example not packing up the groceries correctly. She seemed to be frustrated all the time, perhaps with her own life. This made it very hard for me to really know boundaries in general and in relationships. This is why I moved away from home to train as a nurse at the age of eighteen. It was mum who coerced me into returning near to them after only a few years away. Luckily I found my own place to live. Unfortunately mum became more controlling as I got older. My friends noticed that both her and my sister were phoning me up every day to find out where I was and who I was with. Romano (2016) said that daughters of emotionally unavailable women often have 'imposter syndrome' where you think you are not good enough so consequently suffer from co-dependency. Mum may have felt abandoned as a child as she had to grow up fast when her own mother died and she had to take on the responsibility of looking after her siblings. Also mum got married at a young age and had my sister and me while also very young. Perhaps now she felt that her purpose had gone when we grew up and didn't really need her anymore.

Chapter Four
My Career

I THINK I WANTED TO BECOME A NURSE SINCE I WENT INTO hospital after my accident as a child. Nursing wasn't easy for me, not that it wasn't intelligent enough. During my nurse training, and on my first placement, I was on a ward where the staff were not very nice to me as they noticed my right arm was shaking at times when I was nervous. I felt so nervous and afraid they even made me have my breaks on my own so I had no-one to talk to while they went into the staff room together. I am pretty sure that I was bullied there, and as a consequence it affected myself esteem.

For example the junior ward sister was teaching me to give an injection. She watched me so intently it felt uncomfortable and it made me think they wanted me to fail. I performed the procedure perfectly so she could not fail me. I felt very nervous but I followed her instructions to the letter. She even admitted afterwards that the ward manager had wanted me to fail so she could get rid of me but because I had done it correctly the ward sister could not fail me. However, the ward Manager reported me to the School of Nursing because she thought I was a danger due to my arm shaking. I was heartbroken and did not know what to do. I told my parents and they came to my rescue. They came to support me and they arranged a meeting with the ward sister and the Director of Nursing, and the Clinical Nurse Teacher. Following this meeting I was referred to a neuro surgeon to see if he thought I could continue nursing. The neuro surgeon could not understand why I was referred to him, and saw no reason why I could not carry on. After his assessment and my CT scan, he wrote to the Director of Nursing saying he did not see any reason why I couldn't carry on my training. I remember him saying to me I wish there were more nurses like you dedicated to the job. I was allowed to stay and the next ward placement was so supportive it gave me more confidence.

After a couple of years I moved to Blackpool as a State Enrolled Nurse and made a lot of good friends, two in particular. I used to have a good social life in Blackpool. Four years later I decided to move to Bristol and did an orthopaedic course for enrolled nurses, then a conversion course to convert to a registered nurse. Then I took the orthopedic course for registered nurses. I was really happy in Bristol so I wanted to stay there and have a place of my own. So I looked at a flat in Weston Supermare and I was excited about it until mum came down just before I was going to sign the contract for the flat, my mum asked me how can you live so far away from your mother. I of course did not want to hurt her feelings so I looked for a job closer to my family. This put pressure on me to do what she wanted and neglected my own needs. I did not consider my own needs as important, by ignoring my own needs I became oblivious to what I really wanted.

I then worked at the large inner city hospital in Manchester for nine years. While I was here I commenced the nursing diploma to better myself but however at the same time I was forced by the nursing management to also commence other courses called teaching and mentorship in nursing, and high dependency nursing. I wasn't aware at the time just how overloaded I was. At the same time I was holding in a lot of pain about a broken relationship that I thought was going to be special. I heard my inner voice telling me to slow down but I did not know how to. I was totally exhausted taking on these courses and trying to heal from my heartbreak over Carl (see chapter 5). I didn't know any better so I just carried on like I always did ignoring the pain.

When I was at work I could fully concentrate on the tasks I was performing and I could keep myself busy. I was constantly on the go. Business and being out of control has been described as over identification with rajas (rage) as we become agitated and confused we feel we are under great stress. We cannot find peace or rest. Our attention is scattered and business cannot be sustained indefinitely.

Your actions become inefficient and you become prone to making mistakes. (Notes from the School of Philosophy Northwest). I can see how my fear and sadness had created an extremely anxious person.

Eventually it occurred to me that I needed a new direction and a new challenge in life therefore I looked for a new job. I saw a nursing post for a staff nurse in an intensive care unit in another large hospital in Salford and decided to apply. This was a very challenging job where I was a bit afraid too. While there I completed the critical care course which enhanced my nursing skills greatly. During my time there I never had any relationships with men as I had shut my heart up to love and the painful memories. I didn't want to get hurt again so I denied myself feeling love. I do think the 'patterns' of any relationship would still be the same as before as I carried so much fear.

Unfortunately I still felt I was not good enough as I received bullying from one of the senior sisters about my shaking hand. Again the experience of my right hand shaking reared its ugly head. She said I was going to be a danger to the patients so once again I had to defend myself as I had done before. Raking up feelings of being inadequate. I worked here for sixteen years before making the mistake of taking early retirement due to a stressful episode where my brain took on too much. Prior to this I was very happy here and made a lot of lifelong friends. Leaving work when I did not want to and as I was reaching the age where I could retire young if I wanted to. I did not actually want to leave fully. I had discussed it with one of my old friends who had retired and she said how good it was to have more time and less stress. It was different for my friend as both her parents had died and she inherited money, her mortgage was paid off and she was now financially secure. I could not really afford to retire completely so I decided to change to a part time role. I did not want to upset my friend by mentioning her parents had died. I hadn't yet paid off my mortgage so I needed to work on until I was financially comfortable. I was comparing myself to her and she seemed very happy. She no longer had other responsibilities and she was totally free, whereas I didn't feel free and felt trapped. I enjoyed being part time, however this meant that I could not keep up with the demands of the changing environment. It was important to me. However, I carried on until there was an event that changed everything. It was due to feeling that I had made a mistake at work and this compounded the mistake I had made with Carl by not being able to be true to myself. I also felt I had to take more responsibility for looking after my parents and my sister. My sister had been made redundant at the time and was very depressed about it, especially as my parents were demanding more of her time to run them here and there. Being dysregulated means your brain is not working with your heart.

The Stressful Event At Work

One day there was an incident at work when a colleague's patient became desaturated of oxygen and she asked for my advice. I assessed her patient and he began to desaturate even further. I decided we needed more help and pulled the emergency cord to summon help. When help arrived instead of them helping me they were all shouting my name and saying Rachel what shall we do.

There were several doctors and nurses around but they were shouting my name. I became overwhelmed and could not think straight, even though I knew what to do I just froze. The nurse whose patient it was had disappeared to God knows where. Fortunately the patient recovered well from this episode. I felt as if I had not been enough and felt ashamed because I had gone into 'freeze mode' even though it was not my fault. It was obvious that my brain was not functioning well because I was stressed even though I knew what to do but could not express myself and my brain was trying to work too many things out. I felt it was all on me and I took the blame. I took it personally and this finally made me think I was no good at my job and I needed to leave. This is part of the imposter syndrome where you do not think you are good enough. Imposter syndrome has been discussed on page 8 (Romano 2016). I then acted out of impulse and gave in my notice. Both my managers asked me to really think about it but of course I couldn't think straight about anything. They seemed to be in shock at my decision and could not understand it. I told them I did feel that I did not make any difference working there but the managers said yes you do make a difference.

My brain was so dysregulated that I was saying yes when I meant to say no I don't want to leave. Even on my last day in the job I wanted to say I think I have made a mistake but I never did. I had an opportunity to go back and do some work in the follow up clinic on a voluntary basis but did not take it up. This was because of my negative thinking.

Chapter Five

Falling In Love With An Emotionally Unavailable Man

WHILE I WAS WORKING AT THE LARGE HOSPITAL IN MANCHESTER on the orthopedic ward is where I met Carl who was a patient on the ward. He was a very attractive young man in his late twenties. Tall, dark and handsome and very charismatic, and I just thought wow who are you. As soon as he passed me while I was working at the nurses station I thought oh my goodness he is so beautiful and my heart started racing and my stomach had butterflies. I just felt that I had met the man that I was going to marry. I was so excited and I just wanted to get to know him better. I started to go to work much earlier than I needed to just to get to know him and just to look at him and have a chance to talk to him. Was I becoming attached to someone I couldn't have? Halpern (2004) said there is a level of love called 'hunger attachment' when you are addicted to another person that is so powerful that it completely overrides practical considerations like 'red flags'. I did not know at the time that Carl was going through a divorce. This attachment could be called 'limerence' like you are walking on air as you become obsessed by someone. I mentioned to a colleague how much I liked Carl and she actually telephoned him and told him it was me who liked him. He then returned the call to the ward and spoke to me so I thought he must have liked me too. I suggested it would be nice to meet up and so we arranged for me to go to his house, to get to know each other. After our first encounter at his house he said he would like to see me again. We then exchanged telephone numbers and asked me to ring him. I think at first I was trying to take our relationship calmly but when he said "you have met the right man" part of me wanted to say I think I should find out for myself. Secretly I wanted to believe it, but it felt like something he would say to a lot of women. Carl began saying lots of things to me that I had never heard of and it was upsetting me. "Do you like lots of love? This sounded like a temporary gesture; like I was being taken into 'Willy Wonkers' factory and being asked if I like sweets because you can have it all this week but next week you can't have it, as he will be giving it to someone else. Perhaps I should have asked him what he meant. Then I thought oh don't be like that he might be genuine. This kind of attachment is very strong stuff and can out last and overshadow limerence and your judgement. It could be very coercive and can make you stay in a relationship that may be bad for you. Or perhaps I should have just listened to my heart.

Our first evening out was brilliant and I felt at peace. He seemed very nervous. I wanted to reassure him that I was there to see him and get to know him better. During our conversation he told me he was getting a divorce and my heart sank. I just wanted to say well lets just enjoy this evening together. At the end of the night it was time to go home and Carl asked to see me again. He gave me his telephone number and asked me to give him a call. When I got home I thought how lovely he was. I was still so excited about him I phoned him the next day even though I was unsure whether or not to ring him. In the end I decided I would and he seemed glad to hear from me. Maybe I should have waited for him to phone me? He asked me how I felt about him but I didn't know what to say. Actually I really wanted to say I was head over heels about him but didn't. He repeated that "you have met the right man". However, I remained silent for ages until he said "I don't mean to put you under any pressure". Perhaps I should have asked what he meant by that. A voice inside of me wanted to say you are rushing my feelings and again that it feels like you are saying this to lots of women, especially as you are getting a divorce it sounds very needy. In fact he had also said are you excited? Which I thought was a very strange thing to say and shows a little self entitlement which could also be said to be a trait of narcissistic behaviour. I wanted to say please think about what you have just said and phone me back when you have. Yet I did not say anything as I wanted to protect his feelings. I felt he was spoiling the relationship before it began and I was really looking forward to getting to know him. Of course, I never said it as I did not want to hurt him. Carl made me feel rushed and under pressure to say how I really felt and I was caught off guard. I even saw a red flag but ignored it as I did not know what it meant.

Howard (2023) suggests that we hide our emotions as a means of defence. We care for others but not ourselves. It is our emotional body's intelligent way of protecting ourselves. The harder we push people away the stronger they become in pushing back what we resist will persist. By saying what I wanted to say it would have given us both time to think about our relationship.

I was smitten with Carl and wanted to pursue the relationship without really knowing him properly. I could see a potential relationship but my fear and anxiety got in my way of exploring it any further.

I asked whether he thought his wife would want to come back to him?, as I was unsure at that point. This made me question if I was doing the right thing by being with him, and did I need to step back. However I wanted to continue seeing him as he made me feel excited. His response to this question was an angry one so I did not question it further. The next day I telephoned him to say how much I enjoyed his company; he then asked me how I felt about him. He said again I think you have met the right man. This made me feel rushed and under pressure to say what I really felt about him and so I stayed silent. He then said I did not mean to put you under pressure. This made me feel even more under pressure making me feel like it was a well rehearsed line that he might say to a lot of women. I was caught off guard and I could not cope with the situation. I wanted to express how I felt but I did not want to appear vulnerable. However (Bradshaw 1998) says that intimacy requires vulnerability and lack of defensiveness but due to my fear I was too defensive and unable to show my love to Carl. I felt ashamed because I felt I was being rushed and I must have come across as uncaring and insincere. A voice in my head was telling me to tell him how I really felt but I couldn't.

It was coming up to my birthday so I suggested that we go out for a meal. He agreed and he went to a lot of effort to arrange transport and a reservation at a lovely restaurant. We had a great time but in the back of my mind I was thinking, do you bring a lot of girls here? This was probably due to my over-thinking, which is one of my big problems. I realise now how inexperienced I was in the matters of the heart, but my ego pretended otherwise. I arranged to meet again at my suggestion. This is chasing love which I did not understand at the time, (Roxanne 2024) "recognizes that 'when we turn a blind eye to the warnings from our intuition then we do ourselves a huge disservice. We are betraying our higher selves".

My mistakes:

1. Telephoning Carl first.
2. Putting his needs before mine.
3. Not listening to my gut feelings.
4. Not saying how I felt and not being authentic.
5. Chasing him out of fear.
6. Had too much sattva - feeling like you are in ecstasy but don't consider other peoples' needs. (One of the three

gunas from Hinduism). This can also be your ego and your shadow (jung 1916)

Virtue (2013) suggests that as a passive person you hold in your feelings as you don't want to hurt anyone. She describes these types of people as 'Earth Angels'. Earth Angels will also try to protect you from toxic or abusive relationships and this must have been the red flag that I saw. I ignored his questions as I knew it felt dangerous. I guess Carl made me feel unsafe so much that I could not say the words I wanted to say to you. Words got mixed up in my head. Sometimes I look back and I don't even recognise the person I was then. It was like I had become quite manic. This behaviour has been explained as the flight or fight mode. I was literally fighting my feelings for Carl but was too scared to say anything. I just said I was not aware of my behaviour when really I wanted to say I am petrified and I do not feel safe, even though he was my heart's desire. It was so hard. I should have listened to the universe and let things happen instead of forcing things. Perhaps in the end because of my nerves I must have come across as uncaring, however it was a mirror to his behaviour towards me as he seemed right.

Perhaps I was as they say 'love bombed', even though I had never heard of that expression before. Why does it happen, why don't you see the signs and why don't you trust your gut instincts? Perhaps it's a desire to be loved by this person. (Kelley 2024) says it's more than a crush, it's an addiction and that you feel you're in love. They rush your feelings; but it's all about their own interests. Because this person knows you desire them they could be called 'players' and they are usually unreliable. They often have many partners and loyalty is not in their character. Kelley goes on to say that this addiction can cause a rush of hormones, especially if you have romantic thoughts. This can be followed by gas-lighting or even depression. Players can devalue you and this can cause low self-esteem. I hope Carl did not think I was love bombing him but I sincerely hope that's not how he felt. If he did think that it was truly unintentional. Carl's rejection hurt me like hell. It certainly had a detrimental effect on my life. Perhaps Carl was sent into my life as a 'shadow', a mirror image. According to Buddhism people are sent into your life for a reason. It's about learning lessons in life. Unfortunately it has taken over thirty two years and the loss of a house, and a loss of my real feelings. Carl seemed very casual during our later conversations, however he invited me to a wedding evening reception with him on the following Saturday as he had nobody to go with. My gut feeling was telling me he was only using me, but I ignored it. I could not go to the wedding as I was working on an early shift the morning after. I phoned him again later because I felt I had let him down but this was a big mistake. Carl asked me if I wanted to go out the following Saturday with his friends. Because I had let him down the week before and didn't want to hurt him I agreed even though it was not convenient due to my shifts and I thought it would be nice to meet his friends. When I arrived at Carl's house he was clearly annoyed because he said "oh it's you; you are too early", and went upstairs leaving me on my own. I did not know what to do. Was I too early?

I was a bit frightened and I wanted the ground to swallow me up. Should I go home? When he eventually came downstairs he looked so nice I told him so. He didn't say anything about the way I looked and this hurt me very much. I went to meet his friends but was surprised to see so many of them, in fact there was a large coach party of them. Carl was so popular with them all whereas I felt like a rabbit caught in headlights. I was so overwhelmed and scared, especially as it seemed he didn't really want me there.

The evening went from bad to worse because of his response to me when I first arrived. He did not speak to me very much apart from saying, when I mentioned the restaurant was nice, he would take me there again if I wanted. Carl did not introduce me to any of his friends. It felt like I was not supposed to be there. I think even his friends were a little surprised. I felt invisible. I wanted to talk to them but I did not know what to say because he had made me feel uncomfortable and a burden. I would have preferred to speak to girls that were there but he took me away from them. Carl did not even ask me if I wanted a drink but some wine appeared on the table from one of his friends. I was too nervous to say I did not want to drink too much alcohol. I mentioned that his friends seemed to think the world of him and he said he thought the world of them. In my head I wanted to say I would like to say that to you too, but I was too afraid. I wanted to ask him if we were real as it felt like I was in heaven but somehow it didn't feel real at all. Halpern (2004) described this as an addiction to a person that makes you feel on cloud nine. She also mentions that a love relationship requires two people. However being in love requires only one. Whilst we were watching the karaoke his friends were going to leave for another place around the corner. Carl clearly wanted to go with them and asked me to go with him too. I wanted to watch the people singing as I was enjoying it but as it would be rude to refuse I went with him. I was still feeling tense and afraid. There were lots of his male friends asking Carl "whose this then", and one in particular said "how do you do it mate?" This made me feel very insecure. I thought I must be a joke and I felt like I was in some kind of competition. I was seeing things negatively even though it could have been a positive thing. (another red flag warning). One of his friends said "when are you going to buy me a drink then Carl?"; as he was the one who was buying all the drinks so far. I immediately said "I will buy you one". His friend looked quite surprised and said "are you sure", I said "of course I will". I then asked Carl what he wanted. He said take this money; he eventually got £10 out of his wallet. (another red flag warning). When I had brought the drinks back Carl began to be quite nice and said that I seemed like I had put walls up and when I got so far you clamped up. Was it any wonder? I was in fight or flight mode again. It was very late, actually four in the morning when we finally got home. I was so tired and only had a couple of hours left to sleep. I told Carl I thought his friends were lovely. He replied "they will be your friends too". I wanted to say I would love that but I was too afraid. It was all too much for me. I wanted to say I love you but I was scared, and what is this feeling I have when I am with you? The words would not come out. I for some reason went straight to bed as I just wanted peace. This is because we were both giving each other mixed signals not being nice to each other. I was tired and a bit drunk and I just wanted to lie down. I think Carl wanted me to stay downstairs for a while because when he came upstairs he seemed annoyed with me. I felt so anxious. I hardly had any sleep and when the alarm went off it felt like I had only just blinked my eyelids. It was now only 5am and so I wondered why he got me up so early. I was so tired I fell back to sleep until 6am. When I woke up and saw him I might have said something he misinterpreted and he replied "you bloody what!". I then became so afraid of him in that instance. Just when will it get better.

I rolled over and wanted to cry. Nothing happened between us that night. He must have thought I was desperate but I just wanted peace. We had not been intimate or loving towards each other. Let me just say I do not think we were very kind to each other. Carl was still clearly annoyed as I think he wanted more but I just couldn't respond due to my tiredness and anxiety. I don't think he wanted me there now. I was met with silence on leaving. I must have hurt his feelings but he was scaring me.

I think we were both 'trauma bonded' (see page 30), and didn't really get to communicate our feelings. I phoned him up later that day and he was quite different to me. I was over-explaining myself which is clearly a sign of being emotionally exhausted. The saddest thing about it is that he said he wanted to get to know me and had exactly the same feelings I had about him in the beginning. All the things I have mentioned are bad timings. Carl was so clearly emotionally unavailable and I think I was too. I was being kept like a child by my mum, too afraid to take risks and say what I wanted to say and live my own life. A few days later I received a letter from him. He said it was going too fast paced and best of luck. I was annoyed with him because I felt he was to blame, not me. I was devastated although kind of expecting it. I wrote back to him but I don't think he received it. I wanted to mend our relationship but I did not know how. It would have been like putting a sticking plaster on a massive wound; it just won't heal. I wanted to tell Carl "well it was you that was rushing my feelings" but I took all the blame so he wouldn't feel too bad for hurting me. He did not know how hard it's been for me to fight my feelings for you. I wanted to say I just want to be myself but the words never came out and when I said something really foolish you thought I was manic. Well I clearly was as I couldn't explain myself properly. I have been punishing myself for saying the wrong things for ages and for not saying how I really felt and being my authentic self. O'Morain (2018) says to stop sabotaging yourself you need to give yourself some kindness. When I was traumatised about selling my house I remember the doctor saying be kind to yourself. I asked how do you do that then? I made many mistakes that I now realise was through fear. When I look back I know Carl made me feel unsafe and it made it hard to get the right words out. I do not even recognise the person I was becoming, I was different then and I did not like myself. It later led to self hatred and total dislike of myself.

I had fallen in love with Carl instantly but I did not realise at the time that he had become my karmic teacher. The relationship made me realise that I had a fear of getting close to somebody. Halpern (2024) in his book describes that when we feel we are not enough we become the person we need to be to fit in another person's world. We then become our "idealized selves" and it's not our true selves at all. We also can have many personality traits such as helpers. We feel we have to meet the needs of others such as perfectionists or high achievers to fix things to make them right. Howard (2023) describes such personality traits as appearing as a controller, and you find it hard to show any vulnerability, even the traits as a peace keeper makes you reject your own needs as you do not like conflict.

Many years later I wrote Carl a letter again to ask him how he was and how life was treating him but apparently he did not receive it as I addressed to his place of work. I wrote to him again several years later to ask him how he was but had not got this letter either as he had moved house. I was still grieving for Carl even though I wasn't really aware that it was this that was making me feel so sad. Virtue (2013) says that 'Earth Angels' are nice people that cannot recognise a toxic relationship and you defend that person and take all the blame. They also tolerate abusive relationships through fear of being wrong or judged.

Trauma Bonding

How does childhood trauma manifest itself in adulthood? Perhaps both Carl and I were going through our own traumas' and that could be the reason why I felt so overwhelmingly attracted towards him. (Bingham 2025) says that when we are out of touch with our true essence we are like a ship with a proper compass; unable to plot a safe place to navigate towards. I could not think straight because of the fears that were being presented to me. However my real self was really aware of what was happening.

1. He told me "I have found the right man". I thought I would rather like to find that out for myself.
2. He told me he was going through a divorce (red flag alert; a dangerous man at this time and perhaps emotionally unavailable).
3. He was too attractive. He could get anyone he wanted so why would I feel safe with someone like that.
4. Why did he ask me to phone him? Should he not say I'll phone you.
5. What is the reason why he is getting divorced after only three years of marriage? Is he safe for me?

Perhaps my feelings were right. He is a womaniser.

Chapter Six

Twin-flame
Karmic teacher

WHAT DOES THE TWIN-FLAME MEAN? I HAD BEEN WATCHING YouTube and listening to Carl Jung and Buddhist quotes. Twin-flame is someone who comes into your life as a connection that is so overwhelming that it can make you see yourself as you truly are and reflect the parts of you that are needed to heal. It is very powerful. I believe that Carl opened up something in my life that I needed to heal. Once again I pushed my feelings down and pretended it did not matter. I even took his pain so he didn't feel guilty about hurting me. I became the person who he obviously thought I was, but that was not really me and inside I was screaming to myself why can't you get your words out of what you really want to say. It was all because of fear. Why did I become so addicted to him? Whitfield (1991) describes that when we become addicted to things it's a form of co-dependency. We look elsewhere for happiness that is outside our true self and we neglect our needs. This is why I formed dysregulated relationships and thought other people's needs were more important than my own. Whitfield (1991) says it seems like a big payoff by reducing our feelings as we have a fear of those in authority; be it parents, government or organised religion. We have so much fear that we want to help others that it becomes detrimental to ourselves. Co-dependency comes from trying to protect our true feelings as we are vulnerable and delicate, but it can also be powerful. It is an emotional disorder, however it can heal through a process of self responsibility. If we deny ourselves our true self we become our false self which is habit forming. If we become our true self we will become happy. It also says it's an escape from the pain of everyday life. I did this a lot with my family because I did not want to say how I really felt. I could not control my emotions and it became the reason for my emotional pain. Whitfield (1991) also says "You need constant approval from mothers that you become unhealthy and try to people please all the time". I think my intuition was trying to guide me into believing in myself but I just could not do it.

Control and Being Controlled

We were a very small family. My mum, dad, my sister and me. My mum was controlling and wanted to know everything, where people were, who they were with, and what they were doing. I know it was form or caring but it felt quite smothering. I think she wanted to look after me even though I was grown up, she still kept me as a child. Mum even did this with dad, so much so he liked spending his free time doing what he wanted, but this left mum on her own making my sister and me feel guilty. Unfortunately this made me feel like I was in a trap. If I wasn't in at certain times when she phoned, she would then phone my sister to find out if she knew where I was. I was afraid of visiting people in case I upset mum. When I visited someone, especially in the evening I would rush home because she would be worrying about me. This led to even more anxiety in my life. I felt paranoid about this because it made me think I could not be in control of my own life. In addition to this my sister would accuse me of ignoring her if I did not answer the phone immediately when it rang. She made me feel worse and made me feel even more stressed. I did not realise at the time that my sister was also being put under pressure by our mum to find out where I was.

Wikipedia (2021) states that narcissism is a personality trait that involves an excessive focus on oneself and one's needs, often at the expense of others. Narcissism is a diagnosable personality disorder which I think my mum displayed quite a few traits of. I think mum was rather a vulnerable narcissist, even though she was not officially diagnosed with it. To maintain their self-esteem, and to protect their vulnerable true selves, narcisses seek to control others' behaviour, particularly that of their children, who they view as extensions of themselves.

Gas lighting is also a type of control that I realise has been happening to me all my life. The Oxford dictionary (2025) states that gas-lighting is a form of manipulation and can make you feel like you're insane. Examples of what people say when they are being gas-lighting you are 'that never happened',' you're overreacting' and 'you're too emotional' and this can lead to losing your confidence and which can make you numb your feelings and emotionally shut down.

My Sister

My sister and I grew up being quite close to each other. There was only eighteen months in age between us, me being the oldest. For some reason I thought it was my responsibility to look after her. When she felt bullied at school she would tell me and I would sort it out for her. She was able to have long term relationships whereas I struggled with those. I always thought it was more important for you to have a steady boyfriend so that I would feel safer. One time she stole a boyfriend from me when I was working in Bristol and even though I think my relationship with him would not have worked. It still felt like a betrayal and it hurt because I finally found out that her and mum had kept it secret. I always was afraid of having a boyfriend before my sister in case she would become jealous and take him off me. Strangely I did not want my sister to be on her own. I wasn't allowed to be angry with her as mum said "I was upsetting her and bloods thicker than water". I just swallowed my pride and accepted it.

I think I began to compare myself with her and felt she was so much prettier than me. Did this contribute to me sabotaging my relationships? How could anybody be in love with me? I suppose I didn't give them a chance. I needed my sister to be happy so I could relax. My sister once accused me of trying to split her up with a long term boyfriend. She was so mad with me even though I was only trying to protect her. She actually boxed my ears and burst my ear drum. I think I had given her power over me then; it made her more important than me. I had given my power away and lost all control. I do not think she was really aware of how she affected me. Her temper was just like mum's and I was living in fear of both of their reactions. Slowly the joy was being taken away from me. When I was frustrated and fearful about selling my house she couldn't understand why I was so upset. She said I was very selfish and only thought about myself and my dog. She also accused me of crying all the time and for not being able to make decisions. I could not even breathe properly and it felt like there was a lump in the centre of my chest. It was so difficult to breathe. However, she bought me a book on breathing techniques. Jung (1916) describes this as "emotional pain and sadness". I tried other exercises by joining pilates and yoga classes in the evenings but she said I should not be going out at night; blimey it was only five minutes away but I felt I was not even allowed to do that. I was so stressed that I felt I wasn't allowed to do anything I wanted to do.

To keep things stable I used to invite my sister to come with me when going out with my friends. It did not always turn out well as she would be very angry with me and accuse me of ignoring her if I was talking to my friends more than her. I spent most of the time trying to calm her down. She was even critical about where we were going and what we would eat. My friends did notice her behaviour but they did not always say anything at the time. I was always defending her behaviour.

One day during a particularly cold winter the weather forecast was that there was a chance of snow, and only a chance, the following day when I was due to go to work. Mum rang me and said she was worried about it and that I should not go into work. I thought I had managed to convince her that I would be fine but she had rung my sister who then rang me and shouted at me. "You had better not go to work tomorrow, and don't you dare upset mum". However much I tried to say I would be fine she continued shouting at me and said I should consider mum. I tried to explain that my job is not like an office job and would have consequences on the work load of my colleagues if I did not go in. My sister was frightening me so much with her accusations and threats I felt that I had no choice but to phone in sick. This made me feel so ashamed of myself and guilty because I wasn't sick at all. I was torn because I did not want to hurt my mum or my sister but on the other hand did not want to let the hospital down either. I felt so bad because of the fear within me to not experience any conflict with them as they both had such volatile and unpredictable tempers. This led me to say that I would look for a house near her and mum as I felt I had to look after them and totally forgot to look after myself. Also I felt I was not allowed to have a house as nice as my sisters and I tried to make my own lovely house bad so I didn't like it. I tried to explain to mum that my sister was bullying me but she would not have a word said against her.

My sister has got glaucoma in both eyes but is still able to see as she is using her medication strictly and having regular eye pressure checkups. After a recent checkup when the pressures had gone up she became very hostile towards me. She said she would not come to see me if her eyesight got worse and I had not moved closer to her and our parents. This sounded just like the sort of thing mum would say. Luckily her eye pressure went down again after further treatments.

When my sister was diagnosed with breast cancer at the same time mum was diagnosed with oesophageal cancer and later breast cancer. I helped her wherever I could. I would take her to her hospital appointments and give her reassurance about her treatments. She was not happy with me at all and would say "I never asked you to feel sorry for me", "I never said I need you with me during my cancer treatments", "I don't need anyone", and "I should spend my time with my boyfriend not you". I think this particular anger was down to her anxiety of having cancer. I am glad to say her cancer is being successfully treated and she has recovered well from surgery albeit she still has to have regular checkups.

I am trying to build my relationship with my sister but it will now be a more balanced relationship. We need to live our own lives without interference. My sister and her fiance noted that when it came to looking after mum and dad how strong I was and how I stepped up to the mark to organise all the care they needed. I ensured they received the correct medication, nursing care and arranged the doctors visits etc. I especially wanted mum to be as comfortable as possible coming to the end of her life. My mum, dad and sister relied on me entirely.

My sister and I are getting along a bit better now and she has apologised for her treatment towards me. Even though I forgive her, I find it very difficult to forget. I just needed help but how can people help you if you are not honest with yourself?

Covid and how it affected my relationship with my family

I had been away from nursing for about two years when Covid arrived. I felt an overwhelming need to go back to nursing, this was mainly because I really wanted to help people. I also missed the profession and the teamwork. I had so many skills to offer but a feeling of guilt and shame overcame me because I wasn't there to help out. Watching the television and the news became a source of torture for me as I really wanted to go back to work to offer my help. However I was worried about my dog Bonnie and leaving her alone while I was out working. I didn't want to take her back to her previous elderly owners, as they were both frail; in their nineties. The gentleman was so ill at the time I didn't want to put any further physical load onto his wife's shoulders. In addition to this, the government instructed everyone not to visit people, especially vulnerable people, as Covid is easily spread. I could not take Bonnie to my parents or my sister either as they lived in the neighbouring town to mine. I was worried that if I was working in the Intensive Care Unit

(ITU) I might inadvertently transfer Covid to other people wherever I went. My mind was racing. I was asking people's opinions. However when on the telephone to mum I mentioned to her that I wanted to go back to work. She then told my dad who then came on the phone and said I was making him ill and he made me promise that I would not go back. It actually made me ill and made me feel ashamed of myself. That was another example of control from my parents. I started to catastrophize everything and everything around me became overwhelming. I began to struggle with my emotions and I was in turmoil. I really wanted to go back to work but I didn't want to upset him or let him down so I did not apply to go back. It made me feel very ill so much so I had problems with eating and sleeping. I kept on writing things down like to whom should I be faithful to; my dad or the National Health Service (NHS). My feelings were not even in the equation. Howard (2023) describes how we overgive and say yes to people because we may have come from an unhealthy, or even quite toxic family. I felt responsible for everybody. I was overthinking everything.

Mum's Illness

I think mum had been ill for a long time but she never let on or went to the doctors whenever I asked her to. I noticed she coughed a lot whilst eating and was breathless when exerting herself. Mum would always ignore my concern as she didn't want to know what was wrong. She had always ignored her own health.

She found working in the garden a struggle but would not accept help. I was still living further away from her when my sister told me she had fallen and had taken her to hospital. I felt guilty because I wasn't there to help even though my sister said there was no need for me to be there at that time. The hospital said that she had bruises but was ok and she was allowed home. The radiologist said mum had pulmonary fibrosis and was short of breath but not excessively enough to need oxygen. However a few months later they called her in and said that there was something they were concerned about. This led to mum being referred for a gastroscopy. I went with her for this procedure so she would feel safe. However, after the procedure was finished the surgeon kept us waiting for a long time before discussing my mum's condition. I thought this doesn't look good and I was right. He confirmed that mum had a growth on her esophagus and I knew it was probably cancer. We had to wait until the surgeon informed us which was the best course of treatment he felt she should have. In the meantime she was referred to another hospital for a scan to test her lung function. There was no other treatment ordered following this.

The surgeon who had done the gastroscopy had referred mum to an oncologist and when we got the appointment I took her to see him. Mum asked me what I thought it was that was wrong with her. I had to be honest and I told her I thought it may be cancerous growth but it wasn't known then whether it was benign or not. My mind was racing with all the things that mum might need to have done. The oncologist confirmed it was cancer. Mum just sat there quietly and asked how long had she got? I was surprised to hear how direct the oncologist was in saying six months! How can you be so certain I thought. The McMillan nurse (this is what cancer nurses are called in the UK), said they had caught it early. This did not add up in my head at all. Mum was given three options: radiotherapy, chemotherapy or surgery and had only had a couple of weeks to decide. I in my nursing experience thought my mum was not fit enough for surgery at her age and condition. I could not imagine how an oesophagectomy would go well for her.

Mum was left with these choices but later on was told that only chemotherapy was available as the other options were not actually appropriate.

When I took mum home she told dad and my sister she only had six months to live. It was such a shock they could not believe it. I had thought about moving in with them when I had a nagging feeling that I really didn't want to even though I felt a sense of duty to look after mum. There was no way dad could look after her as he was totally incapable of even looking after himself. Mum accepted chemotherapy but after only a month she stopped having it as she could not cope with it and said what is the point of this and said she did not want it as it made her feel more unwell. Unfortunately mum had neglected herself in the past and had done more so since her diagnosis. Whilst she was on the 'chemo' she was confined to bed because she was so weak. My sister and I visited every day. I would drive over after walking my dog to make sure she was being cared for properly as dad just didn't have a clue what to do. We made sure mum was washed and had something to eat and drink even if it was a little.

At the same time as mum had been diagnosed with cancer my sister was diagnosed with stage three breast cancer. When the surgeon told her of the diagnosis I was so shocked and my reaction was to put my hand to my mouth. The surgeon pulled my sister away from me to near her. The surgeon was thinking about my sister and that my negative reaction would cause her more anxiety. This was like another awful thing happening as my sister's reaction to me was like I shouldn't have done that. Her diagnosis was quite shattering to us all. I was so sad because too much was happening at the same time. It did not help when my sister accused me of being selfish and that I should be ashamed of myself because they both had cancer. That I was only thinking of myself and my dog. Why did I keep making mistakes?

It was not long before mum became really sick. My dad began shouting more at me and then mum as I think he was not coping with any of it. My dad had been ill before mum got ill and was forever trying to make himself even more ill so he would need hospital treatment mostly for constipation and dehydration. He was driving mum crazy and she would take out her frustration on me and my sister. My sister had a partner to talk to, to release her tension whereas I had nobody at home to talk to. Eventually dad was diagnosed with vascular dementia and Alzheimer's Disease. He was very agitated and bad tempered. I feel that mum was afraid and exhausted by it. I was being shouted at all the time because "I wasn't doing enough for the family". I stressed about mum and my sister's and dad's behaviour. I was back and forth to the hospital with dad a lot and felt like I was running on empty. I really don't know how I got through it all, especially with being constantly shouted at.

Mum had been given a care package by the multidisciplinary team however I felt it was appalling and inadequate for her needs. I felt responsible so I had to be there all the time to ensure everything was done right. I also became so stressed with it all. Mum's health deteriorated slowly and she lived for another eighteen months. We did not know how this was as she ate very little and had no energy. My sister and I were doing all the shopping and cleaning for mum and dad in addition to nursing her. Whenever I asked dad to help out by making mum a drink and to ensure she drank it he would accuse me of being 'superior' as I had a lot of medical experience. My mum and my sister relied on me to sort out help from the district nurses, get the correct bed and medication. Also arranged the doctor's visits and hospice care. My sister said that it was amazing how I was caring for her and dad, and was so grateful that they didn't need to think about anything as I had it all in check.

In addition to caring for mum I was moving house to be near to them, and I was too afraid to say how stressed I was. Everybody seemed to require something from me and I just could not cope. I was exhausted and felt I had no choice but to sell my house as mum was so ill and my sister was in a panic. She was agitated and shouting at me all the time. Howard (2023) says that when you are very sensitive any shouting makes you shut down your feelings. My feelings had been so trapped that it has had devastating effects on me and eventually I hit rock bottom when I lost the home I loved. My life could have been so different if I had not been so co-dependent. I was asking everybody else what I should do when I really knew what the answers were. I was too scared to say my heart was breaking.

At the end mum was admitted into a hospice and died a week later. The nurses there said she would often call out our names; we were her world. At least she was at peace now. My dad had become so dependent on my sister and I to spend a lot of time with him. I felt that my life had just been to take care of others and not myself. I was the one having to organise things for dad, mum's cremation etc., my mind was all confused and very stressed when things were not as they should be. I realised how mum had passed down her unhealed wounds to my sister and me. I never felt worthy. Mum's dying wish was that we would look after dad and we reassured that of course we would. However it has come at a great expense to me as I have lost the life I could have had by looking after them and other people and not considering myself at all.

Why Do We Sabotage Ourselves?

We should ask ourselves are we living our own life or are we living the life other people want us to live. By being sabotaged by others we then sabotage our own life. It causes you to become too accommodating for others and you become needy, jealous and angry, and you fear disapproval from people. Kelley (2024) states in her book called 'The Magic of Detachment; How to Let Go of Other People and Their Problems', describes how the mother in the family puts pressure on you so that setting boundaries becomes difficult for you. She also says that you should trust your own instinct, and if something does not feel right it isn't. Depression and anxiety are not feelings. Feelings return you to yourself but depression and anxiety are body snatchers that suck the life out of you, (Doyle 2020) in their book 'Untamed Stop Pleasing and Start Living'. It makes you function on high alert all the time and you run around not knowing what to do. I was going through motions and nobody could tell what was wrong with me as I had felt abandoned. I could not say how I was feeling.

To the outside world you appear normal but inside there is inner turmoil.

When my mum was diagnosed with cancer, my sister was diagnosed with breast cancer, and my dad was in and out of hospital with urinary problems, I felt I needed to move nearer to them and help them more through guilt and fear. However, moving house turned out not to be the wisest decision I have ever made. My sister was always over thinking and anxious the most during that time. She would always say you are not doing enough to help the family, however I was taking my sister to her hospital appointments, and my mum to her hospital appointments. I was also looking after mum at home, spending most of the day with her. I was frustrated with the lack of care she was receiving from the multidisciplinary healthcare team. My dad had also just been diagnosed with early onset Alzheimer's disease. My sister said I had not supported her enough with her diagnosis and choice of treatment. It was all too much. My dad seemed to be very angry with me and accused me of being in my element as I was taking charge of everything. But I had to, because no one else knew what to do. After all she was my mother. My sister told me how amazing she thought I was and she had learnt so much from me, and how I took all the pressure off them.

Constant Criticism

You can get used to rejection and criticism so that you think it is normal. This can lead to low self esteem and creates a hostile environment, and can damage your mental health.

It is a form of emotional abuse and you believe you can never measure up to others peoples expectation and this leads to tension in relationships. The more you are criticised the more you withdraw, leading to perfectionism, and you look for flaws within yourself. My mum would ask my sister to go shopping for them and take her and dad to constant hospital appointments. I felt I wasn't doing enough to help them but felt I had to take the burden off my sister.

Chapter Seven

Symptoms of my behaviour

I BEGAN CRYING ALL THE TIME AND WAS ALWAYS ON THE GO. I was always taking my dog or going to help somebody. I felt I always had to take burdens off my sister and had to look after her. Roxanne (2024) explains how changes in your life can become a struggle. Leading to confusion and disorientation by denying our true feelings and makes you feel angry and prolongs your suffering. It has led me over the years to suppress my emotions and bottle things up. It led me to become anxious about everything. I was scared to say how I felt and became paranoid and afraid of people's reactions. My mother and my sister were the main antagonist and I hated conflict of any kind. I just let them shout at me and pretended it did not matter. Really I just wanted peace however I did not have enough strength to challenge them as I worried about their feelings rather than my own. I became obsessed with things, I must please mum and my sister. In addition to that if I didn't go and visit someone I think they must think that I didn't care about them. It was all about taking my dog out for a walk and I was obsessed with how many steps I was doing. The problem of not trusting my own feelings and emotions meant that I ran away from my problems instead of facing them. This led to me hating myself. This kind of self hatred prolongs suffering (Roxanne 2024). Again remembering my relationship with Carl and the shame I felt by not being my true self. Kelley (2024) describes worrying as a self-defeating behaviour. This played havoc with my emotional health. I displayed lots of erratic behaviour. I could not make decisions for myself and I kept forgetting things, for example where my door and car keys were. I was driving erratically and I felt I was trapped in a circle and could not get out. Howard (2023) explained that when we are in a constant state of fight or flight our bodies become normalized to this so we do not know when there is danger and how to deal with it. One of my friends noted how stressed I was. I was displaying shaking, crying, nervous tremors and I could not breathe properly. I would rock back and forth in the chair and rub my arms and legs without realizing what I was doing. I became bad tempered because I couldn't explain to anybody the feelings of anguish. I was so angry with myself. It did not help when my sister said I was making it all up to get attention. She also said "could you not just pretend to be happy for our mother's sake". Pretending to be happy is one of the worst things you can do to yourself (Howard 2023). It made me so afraid to say I did not want to sell my house and made a big mistake, but I couldn't get my words out. Even my dad commented that I was going to have a nervous breakdown. I was constantly moving and was very restless, constantly looking at the clock. Mum would shout out "look at you, you are always looking at the clock". "It's like you don't want to spend any time with us". I actually couldn't spend time with people at that time that I didn't feel safe with. It has been described as the body telling you that something is not right. I became paranoid and thought everyone was ganging up on me, and I did not feel safe. I stopped going out, and I stopped seeing my friends. I had no energy and couldn't sleep properly. I was waking up early in the morning, watching videos on Youtube, I had no appetite because I was not eating properly and therefore had no energy even to think properly. Physical symptoms of stress are called 'somatism' (Howard 2023). He describes that when you are so stressed you experience many physical symptoms. I think these symptoms were all caused because I felt a bit useless as I had left work and had no plans. I was going to take up dog walking but I realised it would not have fulfilled my needs because I missed nursing. I was no longer working and feeling useless, and because of Covid I became very anxious and agitated. It had made me feel I wasn't being true to myself and doing what I wanted to do. The main thing that made me put my house on the market was because my sister and my parents were strongly suggesting that I find a house closer to them. They said it would be nice if you lived near to us and they kept on showing me houses for sale close to them. I felt under pressure yet again not to let them down because I wanted to please them and make them happy.

I thought I was doing the right thing moving closer to mum, dad and my sister so as to not hurt anyone's feelings.

But when I was looking for an estate agent I couldn't decide who to choose. One of my friends advised me to get at least three quotes but this made me even more indecisive. I was full of fear and I knew deep down it was not the thing I really wanted to do. The estate agent I finally picked made me feel very uneasy. I had an unnerving feeling that I had made a grave mistake which turned out to be true. They were bullies and coercive throughout. In my gut feeling I felt I could not trust them. I ended up ringing them every several times a day because I was so concerned. I even screamed down the telephone that I wanted to change my mind and stay where I was, but they would say things like "you just don't like change, and things will be better". "Things will always work out", even though I felt in my gut they wouldn't. I was met with aggressive answers to my worries and that I could not find a house as nice as the one I already had. The response was "just get a move on", and "you think your house is so beautiful", so I felt I wasn't allowed to live there anymore and I now had no choice but to sell. This made me even more ill. They did not have my interests at heart. I felt a lump in my throat and pain in my chest and the words would just not come out. Jung (1916) in (Snowdon 2017) described it as emotional pain as grief because of the things you have denied yourself. It was also described as the 'shadow', this is the unconscious part of your personality that contains the weaknesses that show the aspects you cannot handle. Combined with my sister's anger at me and the aggressive nature of the estate agents pushing the sale it made me extremely agitated and anxious.

And fearful of disappointing people I did not find the strength to say no. My mum even said these people are not your friends, they are business people. However my sister became even more angry and made me question my decision so the following day I put the house back on the market.

Why was I so unhappy about this decision? Maybe it was simply because I did not want to do it and I was too emotionally exhausted with all the pressure from everybody, my brain hurt. I felt trapped. I knew there was something wrong with me but I was too afraid to admit I needed help.

I felt that the couple that the estate agent put forward to buy my house were untrustworthy and were constantly criticising my house to get me to lower the price. I was so stressed and frustrated and weak I just gave in. The estate agent rang me to tell me there was a good offer on the table, but the offer was £5000 below my asking price. I thought that this was not a good offer and I just said no, however my sister who was with me at the time laid into me shouting "that is a good offer and it's a lot of money and you just don't like the town where I live" and where I felt I had to move to. "You don't like this town and you think we all live in rubbish houses", and "you think my house is rubbish". I never said or thought anything of kind, in fact I said "your house is very nice". I finally plucked the courage to write a letter to the estate agents to tell them I wanted to withdraw from selling my house. I wanted to say these people are not welcome in my house as they are devaluing it by criticising it and I wanted them to get lost and find somewhere else to live. My mind had become weak and I gave up. However I made the mistake of taking it to the office in person. One of the female staff said “oh you’re giving your notice in”, and this made me feel bad and weighed on my mind that I let them down. I felt so afraid because I had signed a contract with them in my house with two of the male estate agents, and felt under pressure even though my heart was sinking that I did not have a choice but to carry on with them. Even my sister kept on telling me you have to do it, you have to be brave. I forced myself to be brave and keep face but I did not feel well at all. I put my thoughts aside as I did not feel important enough. With my sister’s voice echoing in my head, torturing me, saying I was going to get a reputation with the estate agent so I just continued with the sale. I kept telephoning the estate agents saying I can’t find any property as nice as where I lived then. The response was you will find a house you like and everything will work out but in my mind I knew I wouldn’t. I think the estate could tell something was not right with me as I was pacing up and down in their office. Is it normal to be upset about selling your house? I wanted to scream but my voice was frozen. I also felt that the estate agents were keeping secrets from me. They did say “we make the decision whether to sell your house, it’s up to us”. They would telephone me and say I had something wrong with my roof and the survey however would not not say what it was. I want to speak to my solicitor but there again they said I wasn’t allowed to. I felt I was trying my best to help them to sell my house even though it was destroying me. This was a big mistake and I knew that in my soul, but I felt so powerless. I remember screaming down the phone at them for fifteen minutes. I was thinking in my head, don't take my house away from me but I could not get the words out. Their response was you just don't like change. After another viewing the estate agent telephoned me with an offer from a couple who were also offering below the market price. I felt that I couldn't speak to anybody, even mum said "what's wrong, you're braver than what you think you are". Because my mum was very ill at the time I did not want to upset her. The bravest thing I should have done was tell her I did not want to move. I just felt lost and alone. All this ended up with me driving my car erratically and forgetting things like appointments. I was asking other people their opinions about me selling my house but they would only say do whatever you want to do, in reality I just didn't know what to do. The fear of my sisters' anger and the pressure from the estate agents stopped me from halting the sale of my house. I had totally lost control and this was when I became very ill. I had become a victim of my own destiny. I did not have the courage to say no. My sister kept on showing me different houses she thought would be right for me and when I would say I did not like them she would get angry and shout "you think this house isn't good enough for you is it!" If I mentioned how beautiful my house was she would shoot me down saying "my house, my house, nothing nicer than my house". "Oh you are so miserable why can't you put a smile on your face". I just couldn't smile. I knew I was unhappy. I felt sick all the time but kept trying to find a house. In the end she actually did find the house I ended up buying. It was not really what I wanted but because I felt I had lost my mind and had no choice and just wanted peace I went along with it. I did not feel comfortable in my new house: it just didn't feel right. My friends noticed that I was not being myself and realised I needed professional help, however I did not know what to do. I was so worn down I eventually gave in, sold the house and moved nearer my parents. On the last day of being in my beautiful house, that I had worked so hard for I was heartbroken and I knew I had been bullied out of it. Shortly after moving I made an appointment with my GP and this started me off with treatment for my mental health.

Catastrophising

I began imagining all sorts of situations that could go wrong and I became even more paranoid than before. I even fell out with my neighbours about them painting our adjoining fence on their side as I thought stupidly, that they would ruin the fence. I had paid a lot of money for the fence, and thought it wouldn't match my side anymore and it would all have to come down. I even threatened them with reporting them to the police and solicitors as it was my fence and I did not know how to save it. I know now that it was very petty of me but at the time it felt like a massive deal. Dr Julia Smith (2022) says catastrophising makes you think of the worst case scenario's, instead of knowing that you have control of your feelings. You also personalise things and feel that everybody is against you. I was in a constant battle on my own, my head was spinning.

Another example of catastrophising; I was working in town doing some voluntary work and parked my car where I thought it would be safe. After doing two hours of voluntary work I walked back to where I thought my car was but it wasn't there! I remember walking up and down the road several times crying and could not understand where it had gone. It was a keyless car afterall, how could anyone break in? Eventually I had to ring the police and my insurance company. When the police came they questioned whether I had actually locked the car and turned the engine off. I questioned my own sanity. I really thought my car had been stolen. After two weeks when the insurance company had paid me out and had given me a replacement car; the forensic police telephoned me and informed me that my car had been parked around the corner all the time, and had not been stolen. The only finger prints in the car were mine. This caused a lot of laughter when I told everyone what had happened. I also confessed to the insurance company about it and they found it hilarious. Obviously my premiums went up. I really needed a new car but didn't expect to get one this way.

Blame

Rumi, a famous 13th century poet (in: Murat Durmus 2022) said people of the world do not look at themselves and so blame others. I was blaming others for how I felt but I was absolutely stuck in the wrong mind set and needed help. I just did not know what to do or where to go. I did not know I had choices and could have said no. My brain was dysregulated that I was saying no when I wanted to say yes, and saying yes when I wanted to say no. Perhaps I was running away from my problems and responsibilities. I never said no to my sister or my mum, and I felt responsible for their happiness at the expense of my own. I did not think I had any value. I blamed myself for getting things wrong with Carl. I just could not say the things I wanted to say. I was trying to protect his feelings but fear got hold of me and I felt insecure and scared. I think now I had put him on a pedestal and ignored the red flags instead of trusting my gut instincts. I did not understand boulderies. I had all the feelings inside of me but I did not know how to process them. Howard (2023) says we blame others when we are not in touch with our feelings. When we are not in touch with our feelings we end up feeling too much. We rob ourselves of the opportunity to go deeper and take the next step. I think I am an empath; feeling other people's emotions. Howard (2023) refers to an empath as a highly sensitive person as you carry others pains or emotions. "You feel that life isn't fair and people are unkind towards you". I did think that people were betraying me and not playing by the rules. Therefore I was always reactive to negativity, the same as my family really was too. As Howard says in his book "Its Not Your Fault" Empaths find it so exhausting and are quick to become overwhelmed by things. The calling card of the ego is blame or an outward focus.

In contrast the higher self (the true you) takes complete responsibility for itself. Howard (2023) also describes that we become frightened of our feelings as we have learnt to become emotionally detached. This builds walls and becomes our prison. Virtue (2013) states you have to take responsibility for your own life, however I did not know I had choices. She also said you become passive and you do not acknowledge your feelings and you numb the feelings so you no longer care about yourself. This is running away from responsibility and "checking out", allowing others to control you, and you become a doormat. It's like your spirit has been beaten out of you. However your soul is alive and well, ready to be reignited. This behaviour usually stems from childhood where you were teased and punished for speaking up, or from a past life where you have received something very painful. It is almost like I had given power to other people over my life; people such as my own family, Carl and the estate agents.

These people became aggressive with me because I could not make decisions about my personal life.

Co-dependency

Whitfield (1991) described co-dependency as an addition to looking elsewhere for happiness. It is the most common of all conditions where you look outside of your true self. This can materialize into behaviors of experiences we neglect ourselves, self neglect is no fun. We get a payoff by reducing our feelings of joyfulness and our authentic needs. Co-dependency is fundamentally about disordered relationships, reinforced by media, government, organised religion and helping professionals and our relationships with others and ourselves.

Co-dependency comes from trying to protect our true selves which are vulnerable and delicate. It heals through a process of self responsibility. If our true selves are denied we begin to think we are our false selves which become a habit, this is a kind of protection. If we become our true self we become happy. Co-dependency can become very harmful as we become misunderstood. We can push away feelings such as fear, shame and anger. You have so many disorders with emotional balance and controlling things, you cannot set boundaries and you deny your feelings. You can also let somebody else's behaviour affect your own behaviour. It can develop into over reacting in stressful situations. It has been described as a disease that makes you suffer with low self esteem. It is a psychological disorder to complete psychological autonomy developing your self apart from your parents behaviours. Developing compulsive behaviours and needing constant approval from others, can develop unhealthy focus on their needs. It can become a fatal disease of emotional confusion, denying one's feelings and making you become a people pleaser.

I did not know how to love or be loved. I could not recognise if someone was trying to get close to me or not. I survived anxiety and fear; it was all I was used to. I did not know how to control my emotions with people, or how to ask for what I wanted. Usually this type of relationship is with a relative, you feel crazy when around this person and frustrated because one minute they are lovable and next they are disrespectful (Virtue 2013). They are inconsistent with their own emotions and I felt constantly like I was walking on egg shells with them. My body was trying to tell me there was a reason why I was ill because I was not being true to myself. (Romano 2016) described chaotic experiences from her co-dependency where her brain became so dysfunctional that she became overwhelmed with emotions. This is probably why I was always saying no when I really wanted to say yes and vice versa. Romano (2016) also said you should avoid people who cause you stress and are cruel but I couldn't avoid my own family could I?

Chapter Eight

Emotional Abuse

WHAT ARE THE SIGNS OF EMOTIONAL ABUSE?

1. Helplessness - This is something I felt in trusting my own feelings and

   And expressing myself.

2. Hesitation to talk openly - I felt this as I pretended to be okay in stressful situations.

3. Impulsive - I was acting spontaneously without being aware of how I was being treated or how things were affecting me.

4. Confusion - I became so confused by other peoples' decisions and anger.

5. Anger with any apparent cause - I had many anger outbursts but then realised I was in the wrong and would apologise. This was usually when I felt I was being criticised or rushed into making decisions when I had not time to think things through.

6. Sudden changes in behaviour - My behaviour became quite erratic; driving crazily, forgetting things and not being able to make decisions.

7. Emotionally upset or agitated - I became agitated and couldn't relax, relax,

   Sleep or eat.

8. Unusual behaviour - this materialised in me by my sucking, biting or rocking back and forth. I would rock in my chair and was unable to express myself, perhaps through a fear I had at the time.

9. PTSD - I had flashbacks, hyper-vigillence, irritability, confusion and self doubt.

I displayed all of these symptoms. I had become paranoid. This may have been due to the fact that I had been with narcissistic people who took advantage of My kindness and vulnerability.

Chapter Nine

Self Help

Jill Bolte-Taylor (2009) is a neuro scientist who suffered a stroke. She studied the brain and described how you can pull yourself out of pain when you know you have choices.

She described the four hemispheres of the brain that makes decisions for us depending on our experiences. This depends on experiences that if we mainly work on the left hemisphere of the brain they are full of control, and we run out of balance. However we could have pleasure If we concentrate on the right side which is full of joy and possibilities. The right hemisphere lives in the here and now. It is the emotive part. The left hemisphere is full of craving and addiction - wears a mask to protect from pain.

The four hemispheres define your character:-

Character 1 is in the left hemisphere, and is the planner and thinking part.

Character 2 is also in the left hemisphere and acts as the protector. When looking for reactions it remembers the pain from the past and urges you to be kind to it.

Character 3 is in the right hemisphere which is the playful and emotional part. It is immature and does not think about behaviour.

Character 4 is also in the right hemisphere and is the part of wisdom where you learn from your mistakes.

Bolte-Taylor (2009) advises that we should know our four hemispheres and observe ourselves for these traits. The part of you that is not happy should be given play and joy. Remember if you have too much on your plate, like looking after others, you will have no joy. Emotions only last ninety seconds so sit with them and be glad of them, as they are you. When you lose part of your brain (e.g. to a stroke, brain injury) you worry you lose your value. You need to heal the pain from the past. Realise that the trauma you have had is part of your life but it does not define you.

Character 4 learning: you should realise that you are ok so thank yourself for having these experiences. Do not hold yourself back, you can turn them into something else.

It is important to get proper sleep, eat well, exercise more and keep hydrated.

Take a pause and slow down.

Healing myself and going to the Doctor

One of my friends was very concerned about my erratic behaviour and rambling over the telephone, talking gibberish. I was trying to explain myself but my friend said she could not make head nor tail of what I was saying. I had forgotten to care for myself. I did not even realise that I was neglecting myself. She urged me to go to see my doctor and get some help. She kindly offered to accompany me but as I did not want to be a burden to her I declined. However I was thinking I must get myself better as I might lose this special friend of mine of thirty six-years and also my other friends too.

When I finally got to see my doctor I wondered why I was there. As I entered the doctor's office I began to cry. I then began to tell him about all the guilt and shame I felt at not going back to work during the Covid pandemic and also about feeling I wasn't doing enough for anybody. I was trying to explain how I was trying to help everybody. I did not realised that I was emotionally exhausted and was running on empty; constantly giving and not receiving. He listened carefully and said I think you are doing a lot to help people but this did not settle my mind. I was still in floods of tears. The doctor talked to me about post-traumatic stress disorder and explained how he would refer me to the mental health team for assessment and help. Roxanne (2024) said we should accept any help offered. I thought I had to do everything myself as asking for help seems to be weak. He said I should be more kind to myself but in my head I thought about how to do that? In fact most people were telling me not to cry and I was not allowed to express myself.

He also prescribed a short course of antidepressants. I thought I did not understand why I needed these but just knew I was not feeling right. I wanted to tell him lots of things about how my life was at the moment but it did not seem appropriate with the limited time of the consultation. The doctor asked me not to cry as I was leaving the surgery as people might think I had bad news so once again I held back my feelings so nobody would feel concern for me. I was confusing everybody as I was confused myself. I was feeling bullied by events happening and not being able to control them. My brain felt like it was being tortured; feeling like my blood pressure was rising and thinking I might be having a stroke. It had been too much for me. I had to punish myself. I was breaking down and I had no strength anymore.

I had to wait for a long time before getting an appointment to see the mental health team. When I finally got to see them I could not discuss my true feelings because I was wearing a mask and pretending that I was ok. To the outside world I thought I looked normal however my friends told me otherwise later on. I saw the mental health team twice and was told that I would be followed up several months later but I was not seen again by that team once I had moved house. However I was offered counseling by the befriending team that I did voluntary work for before I moved house. While on the telephone with this team I began to cry and told them I did not feel right. Even though they invited me out to different events I could not go as I was too afraid. They then offered me some counseling with their own counsellor. I accepted this offer gladly as I knew I needed to talk to somebody. They told me they could tell I was not well and was stressed by the way I was talking. However I still could not open up to the counsellor what my fear was. I blamed myself for getting things wrong in the past. It absolutely drained me. I was lost and kept taking the wrong path. I was cruel to myself. I had abandoned myself and stopped listening to myself. Complying with mum's wishes had taken away my freedoms. I then started to blame others as I did not know what to do.

My parents and my sister had taken my choices away, especially about selling my house and about leaving work and wanting to go back to work. I was so confused because they were controlling me (including the estate agents) and criticising me. I felt inadequate. I had a sinking feeling in my stomach that I had lost all my strength and became numb. I was told by my sister "can you not pretend to be happy?" I found it exhausting and stressful. I started scribbling notes to myself about how stupid I was, and how people had tricked me into doing what they wanted. My mind knew what was happening but I felt I could not stop it. My mental health really suffered. In fact I had a mental breakdown. I was out of control. I just wanted someone to take my pain away as I did not want to take responsibility for it or where to put it. I learnt from this first counsellor "You are enough" however I did not believe it at the time. I continued with the sale of my house even though it was making me very ill. After I had moved house I started seeing other counselors privately to see if they could help me. I realised I saw too many different counselors, four in fact. It was costing too much money and I was just going over the same things, repeating myself and getting nowhere. Each one of the counselors taught me a different thing about myself. One said you have neglected yourself, another you cannot change the past, another said you have choices but I did not know I had. I have always been around manipulating people and I should stop pleasing other people. Once I got the idea that I could not change the past I started to think about what I can do to make myself better. I realised that the counselors could not understand me fully as I could not explain myself properly. Romano (2016) explains this is because of your own fear and co-dependency. People can become quite frustrated with you as you don't know what you really want; I was too afraid of my feelings. I did not know who I was anymore. Romano (2016) also says that we have to acknowledge that we have been victims in a dysfunctional environment. I did not know the people in the new town I had moved to, however, while I was walking in the woods one day with my dog Bonnie I met a lady who advertised that she did 'retreats in nature'. I decided to experience this. I liked being out in nature and being with other people. However after being in nature we would meet in the pub for refreshments. I remember breaking down and crying whilst sitting eating with this nature group. So perhaps this was the beginning of feeling safe enough to express my vulnerability. This led me to join cocoon retreats with the same lady. I found a place where I felt safe to be myself. This further led me to explore angelic reiki and crystal healing. Shortly after this I started going to empowerment for women's groups. This started to build my confidence. Since then I have started a philosophy course and I am learning how to meditate. Somehow all these things combined have given me more peace and enabled me to make my own decisions. I no longer live to please other people. I have now sold my house and I am hoping to make a fresh start back in the area I had moved from. I no longer feel guilty saying no to people. I simply became the person I should have been without wearing a mask. In practising the angelic reiki has given me more guidance so that every time I get a negative thought I can think more positively and turn it around to a more positive thought. I now do not need to live in fear and I am trying to use the right side of my brain (Bolte-Taylor 2009).

The Empowerment for Women course.

This course is just for women and works with the angels. It is for women who have had some trauma in their life and have started to find a voice. It has made me realise that a lot of people have difficulties and you're not on your own. Crystal healing is learning how to work with crystals and their strength to help get rid of negativity.

Philosophy Course This course has been great for me. It is providing me with more grounding and learning how to pause and stay still. Also how to practice meditation and trust your instincts, and think what would a wise person do.

I am learning how to start with gratitude. It is difficult to feel gratitude when you are full of fear. I realise how much better I am now. I am grateful that my mind is no longer cluttered. I have a voice and I have got the ability to say no and not feel guilty. I can freely make decisions now and make better ones. I do have regrets but I do realise that I did not know how to deal with conflicts and difficult situations as much as I do now. I am grateful that I can find my own path, have my own life, and do not need permission to exist.

Chapter Ten

Letters to my family and Carl

Dear Mum,

YOU HAVE HAD A DETRIMENTAL EFFECT ON MY LIFE. YOU WERE over protective when you really did not need to be. I was able to take care of myself but you could not let the attachment go. I needed to find my own path in life.

When you were extremely ill at the end of your life I think you became the person who you really were. I am sure you were grateful for all the help my sister and I gave you. You would say "oh thank goodness you are here" when we visited you. You look so frightened and dependent on us both. Apparently you would shout out our names when you were in the hospice. Hopefully all the stress had gone out of you and you could be yourself; 'like a little girl who had been lost. I am glad I was able to look after you during your illness, although I found it very stressful all the way. Through it all I think I gave you comfort in the knowledge that you could rely on me and my sister to sort out your day to day needs and the household responsibilities for you. I hope you are at peace now and can finally rest.

Dear Dad,

I don't think you had the best childhood, perhaps you didn't feel loved by your father and this affected your behaviour. This in turn affected the decisions I made in life as well. I was too afraid of hurting your feelings when I promised you that I would not go back to work in the hospital during the Covid epidemic. It made me feel so ill not using my nursing skills to help patients and my work colleagues. I felt guilt and shame for not going back but I made a promise to you and as you know I do not break promises. However you broke your promise to me when I asked you to stop smoking as it was having a bad effect on you and mum's health. You broke it and let me down.

Dear Sister,

I apologise if I am upsetting you by writing this letter and book. Looking back through our lives I do not think your more unwelcome behaviours were all your fault. Perhaps if you hadn't left work albeit through no fault of your own, things may have been different. I don't know for sure, as I still think I would be afraid of you and your temper. You must have been frustrated as I felt that you never made, or took the opportunities you could have done to improve your own life.

Always working in jobs that did not give you fulfillment. Perhaps it was the conditioning we both got from our mother.

Your words would often hurt me; it was like you were mimicking mother's frustrations. I always wanted to look after you but by doing so I neglected my own feelings.

Dear Carl,

I was instantly in love with you. I can't explain why, it just happened and I had no control over it. Perhaps I thought it was love as the feelings I felt were so overwhelming. When you told me you were going through a divorce my immediate reaction was to think that I needed to walk away. I knew it wasn't fair on you and it wasn't fair on me but I just couldn't walk away as I found you so magnetic and kind of magical. I had never felt anything like it before. I was very naive and could not control my feelings for you. I wanted to give you so much love but I was so scared I spoiled it mainly by my poor communication with you and because I couldn't face fear. Your actions told me things might not be the same on your side. I just wish I could have had some faith in myself and the courage to tell you that I had fallen in love with you out loud. I do not blame you for walking away from me as I had become quite neurotic and fearful. I just wanted to say I want to be myself as I felt things had gotten out of hand and I wanted to slow down. It was too much when you said my friends would be your friends. If only I had said what was in my heart that I would have loved that too. I didn't want to hurt your feelings but I didn't know how to respond.

I wish I had come downstairs the last night I saw you and spoke openly and honestly with you. Perhaps you would have seen how scared I was and we could have worked it out together.

I could have asked for God's help as I believe he was talking to me in my time of panic. I will never know if we could have been happy together. I think of you everyday and wish I could have said what was in my heart. If anything since then it has taught me to be myself and not worry if people like me or not.

The thing that hurts the most is the thought that I could never really tell you or show you how I felt properly because I was rushed and the fact that you thought I did not care about you when I really did.

I really do hope you have had a happy life and I wish you all the best.

Positive Thoughts

When my mother died it was bad, it was quite a traumatic and difficult time. To make it worse my dad was denying it had happened. I was rushing around sorting out the arrangements for mum's cremation and getting help for dad's dementia. Suddenly I felt a strange sense of relief as most of the burdens had lifted from my shoulders. I had a voice and realised I could make decisions about my life and I had the power to say no. I am now thinking more clearly and I am beginning to heal. I now know I had the power all the time but because of fear I did not use the power within me.

My advice would be to stop and think before you act. There is no rush (unless an emergency). Just be yourself and all will be well. You don't need to be controlled. If I had been my authentic self I would have different choices in my life. For instance when I first left home to begin my nursing career I could have bought a flat near the hospital where I worked that was hundreds of miles away from my family. Who knows I may have been so much happier than how it turned out. However the way things actually turned out has taught me some valuable lessons.

References

Bingham E, (2025); ***Manifest Your True Essense; Clear Your Blocks, Find Your Joy, Live Your Truth,*** London, Hay House Uk

Bolte-Taylor J, (2009); ***My Stroke of Insight,*** London, Yellow Kite, Hodder & Stoughton

Bradshaw W, (1998); ***A Case Study; Treating Schizophrenia With CBT***, Psychology Wizard.net

Dispenza J, (2012); ***Breaking the Habit of Being Yourself; How to Lose your Mind and Create a New One,*** London, Hay House Uk

Doyle G, (2020); ***Untamed Stop Pleasing and Start Living,*** London, Vermilion (imprint of Penguin Random House)

Gilbert G, (2007); ***Eat, Love, Pray,*** London, Bloomsbury Paperbacks

Halpern H,M (2004); ***How to Break Your Addiction to a Person,*** New York, Bantam Books Trade Paperback

Howard A, (2023); ***It's Not Your Fault***, London, Hay House Uk

Hay L, (1995); ***You Can Heal You Life,*** London, Hay House Uk

Jung C,G, (1916); ***The Psychology of the Unconscious, reprint,*** 2016, Connecticut, Martino Fine Books

Jung C,G, (1959); ***Archetypes and the Collective Unconscious, 2nd Edition,*** 1991, Oxfordshire, Routledge

Kelley L, (2024); ***The Magic of Detachment, How To Let Go of Other People and Their Problems PhD, CPC***, New Jersey, Grow Publications Inc O'Morain P, (2018); ***Kindfullness,*** London, Yellow Kite, Hodder & Stoughton

Oxford Dictionary (2025, Oxford, Oxford University Press

Romano L,A, (2016); ***Co-Dependency-Now What; Its Not You Its Your Programming,*** Colorado, Outskirts Press

Roxanne M, (2024); ***How To Stop Breaking Your Own Heart,*** London, Hay House Uk

Rumi J, Al-Din (2022); ***Drops of Enlightenment (Quotes & Poems)*** M, Durmus, CEO Aisoma AG, Independent publisher

Smith J, (2022); ***Why Has Nobody Told Me This Before?,*** London, Michael Joseph

Snowden R, (2017); ***"Jung: the Key Ideas"; From Analytical Psychology and Dreams to the Collective Unconscious and more,*** London, Teach Yourself

Virtue D, (2013); ***Assertiveness for Earth Angles,*** London, Hay House UK

Whitfield C,L, (1991); ***Co-Dependence Healing the Human Condition,*** Florida, Health Communications Inc, self help books

Wikipedia (2021); ***Narcissism***, Oxford, Oxford University Press

Glossary

Anxious Attachment

The need for constant reassurance

Co-Dependency

Not having your emotional needs met - looking for strong people to help you

Dysregulation

Struggling to control your emotions

Empath

The ability to understand and share feelings of another

Ego

Refers to our self-esteem, can be either inflated or fragile

Emotional Abuse

Pattern of non-physical mis-treatment causes fear and humiliation

Gas-Lighting

Manipulation making you feel insane

Hunger Attachment

A deep longing for emotional connection, stems from low self worth

Imposter Syndrome

Feeling your are a fraud, usually connected to professionalism

Limerance

An obsessive infatuation with someone and it thrives on uncertainty

Mothers Wound

Feels like you are guilty all the time, and you feel like you are carrying burdens

Overloaded

Too much to handle and you become overwhelmed

Somatism

Physical symptoms apparent when you have difficulty with emotions

Stavva

A calm mind and awareness but too much can cause feelings of ecstasy and

Imbalance

Toxic

Something that is harmful or dangerous to health

Twin-flame

Mirroring each other's behaviours

Printed and bound by CPI Group (UK) Ltd, Croydon, CR0 4YY
05/05/2026
02102759-0006